1944

U.K. YEARBOOK

ISBN: 9798852035578

© Drew Presley 2023
All Rights Reserved

INDEX

	Page
Calendar	5
People in High Office	6
British News & Events	10
Worldwide News & Events	21
Births - U.K. Personalities	33
Notable British Deaths	40
Popular Music	43
Top 5 Films	49
Sporting Winners	60
Cost of Living	63

FIRST EDITION

1944

January
M	T	W	T	F	S	S
					1	2
3	4	5	6	7	8	9
10	11	12	13	14	15	16
17	18	19	20	21	22	23
24	25	26	27	28	29	30
31						

●:2 ○:10 ◐:18 ●:25

February
M	T	W	T	F	S	S
	1	2	3	4	5	6
7	8	9	10	11	12	13
14	15	16	17	18	19	20
21	22	23	24	25	26	27
28	29					

◐:1 ○:9 ◐:17 ●:24

March
M	T	W	T	F	S	S
		1	2	3	4	5
6	7	8	9	10	11	12
13	14	15	16	17	18	19
20	21	22	23	24	25	26
27	28	29	30	31		

◐:1 ○:10 ◐:17 ●:24 ◐:31

April
M	T	W	T	F	S	S
					1	2
3	4	5	6	7	8	9
10	11	12	13	14	15	16
17	18	19	20	21	22	23
24	25	26	27	28	29	30

○:8 ◐:16 ●:22 ◐:30

May
M	T	W	T	F	S	S
1	2	3	4	5	6	7
8	9	10	11	12	13	14
15	16	17	18	19	20	21
22	23	24	25	26	27	28
29	30	31				

○:8 ◐:15 ●:22 ◐:30

June
M	T	W	T	F	S	S
			1	2	3	4
5	6	7	8	9	10	11
12	13	14	15	16	17	18
19	20	21	22	23	24	25
26	27	28	29	30		

○:6 ◐:13 ●:20 ◐:28

July
M	T	W	T	F	S	S
					1	2
3	4	5	6	7	8	9
10	11	12	13	14	15	16
17	18	19	20	21	22	23
24	25	26	27	28	29	30
31						

○:6 ◐:12 ●:20 ◐:28

August
M	T	W	T	F	S	S
	1	2	3	4	5	6
7	8	9	10	11	12	13
14	15	16	17	18	19	20
21	22	23	24	25	26	27
28	29	30	31			

○:4 ◐:11 ●:18 ◐:27

September
M	T	W	T	F	S	S
				1	2	3
4	5	6	7	8	9	10
11	12	13	14	15	16	17
18	19	20	21	22	23	24
25	26	27	28	29	30	

○:2 ◐:9 ●:17 ◐:25

October
M	T	W	T	F	S	S
						1
2	3	4	5	6	7	8
9	10	11	12	13	14	15
16	17	18	19	20	21	22
23	24	25	26	27	28	29
30	31					

○:2 ◐:9 ●:17 ◐:24 ○:31

November
M	T	W	T	F	S	S
		1	2	3	4	5
6	7	8	9	10	11	12
13	14	15	16	17	18	19
20	21	22	23	24	25	26
27	28	29	30			

◐:7 ●:15 ◐:23 ○:30

December
M	T	W	T	F	S	S
				1	2	3
4	5	6	7	8	9	10
11	12	13	14	15	16	17
18	19	20	21	22	23	24
25	26	27	28	29	30	31

◐:7 ●:15 ◐:22 ○:29

PEOPLE IN HIGH OFFICE

Monarch - King George VI
Reign: 11th December 1936 - 6th February 1952
Predecessor: Edward VIII
Successor: Elizabeth II

Prime Minister

Winston Churchill - Conservative
10th May 1940 - 26th July 1945

Ireland	Canada	United States

Taoiseach Of Ireland
Éamon de Valera
Fianna Fáil
29th December 1937
- 18th February 1948

Prime Minister
Mackenzie King
Liberal Party
23rd October 1935
- 15th November 1948

President
Franklin D. Roosevelt
Democratic Party
4th March 1933
- 12th April 1945

	Australia	Prime Minister John Curtin (1941-1945)
	Brazil	President Getúlio Vargas (1930-1945)
	China	Premier Chiang Kai-shek (1939-1945)
	Cuba	President Fulgencio Batista (1940-1944) Ramón Grau (1944-1948)
	Egypt	Prime Minister Mustafa el-Nahhas Pasha (1942-1944) Ahmad Mahir Pasha (1944-1945)
	France	Leader of Free France Charles de Gaulle (1940-1944) Chairmen of the Provisional Government Charles de Gaulle (1944-1946)
	Germany	Chancellor Adolf Hitler (1933-1945)
	India	Viceroy and Governor-General of India Archibald Percival Wavell (1943-1947)

	Italy	Prime Minister Pietro Badoglio (1943-1944) Ivanoe Bonomi (1944-1945)
	Japan	Prime Minister Hideki Tōjō (1941-1944) Kuniaki Koiso (1944-1945)
	Mexico	President Manuel Ávila Camacho (1940-1946)
	New Zealand	Prime Minister Peter Fraser (1940-1949)
	Russia	Communist Party Leader Joseph Stalin (1922-1952)
	South Africa	Prime Minister Jan Smuts (1939-1948)
	Spain	Prime Minister Francisco Franco (1938-1973)
	Turkey	Prime Minister Şükrü Saracoğlu (1942-1946)

BRITISH NEWS & EVENTS

JAN

	The PAYE (pay as you earn) system of tax, piloted by Chancellor Sir Kingsley Wood in 1940/41 to replace annual and half-yearly tax collections, is introduced.
12th	Prime Minister Winston Churchill and General Charles de Gaulle begin a two-day conference in Marrakesh, Morocco. During the talks they discuss the co-operation of a French expeditionary force in the Allied invasion of Europe and the setting up of a French Provisional Government.
15th	General Dwight D. Eisenhower, the newly appointed Supreme Commander of the Allied Expeditionary Force, arrives in London to take command of Allied forces and execute plans for the invasion of Europe.
19th	The Royal Navy corvette HMS Violet sinks the German submarine U-641 in Atlantic Ocean. There are no survivors.

21st January: Operation Steinbock, a strategic bombing campaign by the German Luftwaffe targeting southern England, begins. Sometimes called the Baby Blitz, the raids last until May 1944. *Notes: Steinbock was the last large-scale bombing campaign of the war by the Germans against England using conventional aircraft. The Luftwaffe achieved very little during the campaign and lost 329 aircraft before the operation was abandoned some five months later. Photo: Londoners give the victory sign as they sit among rubble of buildings that have been destroyed by heavy bombing in the Nazi air raids over the capital (24th February 1944).*

JAN

21st	The German city of Magdeburg is heavily bombed by the RAF during a raid which destroys much of the city centre. The death toll is estimated at 2,000-2,500.
27th	The Royal Navy light cruiser HMS Spartan is sunk by a Henschel Hs 293 guided missile dropped from a German aircraft off Anzio, western Italy; 46 men are lost.

FEB

8th	The British submarine HMS Sportsman torpedoes and sinks the German merchant ship SS Petrella north of Souda Bay, Crete. The ship, carrying 3,173 Italian internees being transported back to Germany, is targeted despite having been clearly marked as a prisoner of war transport; 2,670 prisoners are killed when the Petrella sinks. *NB: A factor in the high death toll was that the German guards did not open the holds where the POWs were being kept, and fired on those trying to get out.*
15th	Berlin is attacked by 826 British bombers in the largest raid by the RAF against the city to date. In the space of 30 minutes 2,642 tons of bombs are dropped on the German capital; 43 aircraft are lost.
18th	The British light cruiser HMS Penelope is torpedoed and sunk by the German submarine U-410 in the Mediterranean near Naples; 417 of her crew, including the captain, go down with the ship; 206 survive.
20th	Big Week (or Operation Argument), a sequence of raids by the United States Army Air Forces and RAF Bomber Command, begins and continues until the 25th February. Part of the European strategic bombing campaign against Nazi Germany, the Allied actions during Operation Argument allow them to achieve air superiority thus making subsequent bombing raids less risky and more effective.
20th	The Royal Navy destroyer HMS Warwick is torpedoed by the German submarine U-413 off Trevose Head, Cornwall. The Warwick sinks within minutes with the loss of 67 crew; 93 men are rescued.

MAR

10th	The Royal Navy corvette HMS Asphodel is sunk by the German submarine U-575 off the west coast of Galicia, Spain; 92 of the 97 men aboard are killed.
19th	The secular oratorio "A Child of Our Time" by British composer Michael Tippett is premiered at the Adelphi Theatre in London.
20th	While returning from a 300-bomber-raid on Berlin, RAF Flight Sergeant Nicholas Alkemade's Avro Lancaster heavy bomber is hit by a German Junkers Ju 88. The aircraft catches fire and begins to spiral out of control. Alkemade's parachute catches fire so he makes the decision to jump from the aircraft without it, preferring to die on impact rather than burn to death. He freefalls 18,000 feet (5,490m) and loses consciousness. As he approaches the ground tree branches and deep snow interrupt his descent and he amazingly survives the fall. *Follow up: Alkemade spends three weeks in hospital before being sent to the Luftwaffe-run POW camp Stalag Luft III where he becomes a minor celebrity. He is liberated by Soviet forces in January 1945. Note: The rest of doomed Lancaster crew were killed when the aircraft crashed and burst into flames.*

MAR

24th March: The Great Escape: 76 Allied air force personnel attempt to escape by tunnel from Stalag Luft III in Nazi Germany. The escape, conceived in March 1943 by RAF Squadron Leader Roger Bushell and authorised by the senior British officer at the POW camp Herbert Massey, consisted of digging three tunnels, Tom, Dick, and Harry, to try to help over 200 men to their freedom. Harry was ultimately used for the breakout but it was discovered as the escape was in progress. Of the 76 prisoners who broke free 73 were recaptured, 50 of whom were executed, including the leader of the escape Roger Bushell. *Interesting facts: Following the escape the Germans made an inventory of the camp and uncovered how extensive the operation had been. Some of the missing items included four thousand bed boards, 90 complete double bunk beds, 52 twenty-man tables, 10 single tables, 34 chairs, 76 benches, 246 water cans, 30 shovels, 1,219 knives, 478 spoons and 582 forks. In total more than 600 prisoners had been involved in the construction of the tunnels; Harry was built 8½m below the surface and was 102m long. Photo: The German POW camp Stalag Luft III.*

30th	795 British bombers attack Nuremberg, 572 Lancasters, 214 Halifaxes and 9 Mosquitos. A full moon and a cloudless sky make it easy for the Luftwaffe; 95 aircraft are lost (the biggest Bomber Command loss of the war).

APR

14th	The British cargo ship SS Fort Stikine, carrying a mixed cargo of ammunition, cotton and oil, explodes in the harbour at Bombay, India. Thirteen other ships are lost in the explosion which leaves 231 service and port personnel dead, and 476 injured. Civilian casualties are 500+ dead, with 2,408 treated in hospital.

APR

- **16th** — American and British aircraft forces start their bombing campaign of Belgrade, Yugoslavia, targeting railroad marshalling yards, the aircraft industry and the airport. As many as 1,160 civilians are killed in the raid; German military losses number just 18.
- **26th** — German General Heinrich Kreipe is kidnapped outside Heraklion, Crete, by British Special Operations Executive (SOE) agents Major Patrick Leigh Fermor and Captain Bill Stanley Moss (with the support of the Cretan resistance). *Follow up: Kreipe, the head of German forces in occupied Crete, was interrogated and sent to a POW camp in Canada. He was later transferred to a special camp in Wales before being released from British captivity in 1947.*

28th April: During Exercise Tiger, a full-scale rehearsal for the Normandy landings at Slapton Sands in Devon, eight Landing Ship Tanks (LSTs) are attacked by German Navy E-boats (Kriegsmarine fast attack craft). In total 749 servicemen (551 United States Army and 198 United States Navy) are killed. *NB: Because of the impending invasion of Normandy the incident was kept secret at the time. Photo: American troops landing on Slapton Sands during rehearsals for the invasion of Normandy.*

MAY

- **3rd** — Exercise Fabius (the last major Allied rehearsals for the Normandy landings) takes place along the south coast of England.
- **15th** — The final briefing to all the top commanders on the plans for D-Day are held at St Paul's School in London. Those attending include King George VI, Prime Minister Winston Churchill, General Dwight D. Eisenhower, General Bernard Montgomery, and a number of other senior personnel.
- **18th** — After 4 months of fighting the Germans evacuate Monte Cassino and Allied forces, led by Władysław Anders from Polish II Corps, take the stronghold after linking up with the British 78th Division. In total the fighting at Monte Cassino results in 55,000 Allied casualties; German losses are estimated at around 20,000 killed and wounded.

MAY

29th May: A tremendous thunderstorm causes a torrent of flood water to tear down from the high moors through Holme Valley (near Huddersfield) before blasting Holmfirth. Three Holmfirth residents lose their lives; the damage caused is estimated to be between £250,000 and £350,000. *Photo: A collapsed building at Victoria Bridge, Holmfirth.*

JUN

4th	British Group Captain James Stagg persuades General Dwight D. Eisenhower to change the date of the Allied invasion of Europe from the 5th to the 6th June due to unfavourable weather conditions.
5th	Eisenhower gives the go-ahead for Operation Overlord. That evening a letter is distributed to members of the Allied forces telling them: "You are about to embark upon the Great Crusade, toward which we have striven these many months. The eyes of the world are upon you".
5th	At 22h15 the BBC transmits coded messages, including the second line of the Paul Verlaine poem Chanson d'automne, to the French Resistance, indicating that the invasion of Europe is about to begin and that they should begin sabotage operations.
6th	Operation Neptune, D-Day: An extensive aerial and naval bombardment of the coast of France begins. At the same time 24,000 American, British and Canadian airborne troops are dropped behind enemy lines to blow up bridges, sabotage railroad lines, and take other measures to prevent the enemy from rushing reinforcements to the invasion beaches (code named Utah, Omaha, Gold, Juno, and Sword). Hours later the largest amphibious landing force ever assembled begins moving through the storm-tossed waters toward the beaches of Normandy, France.

JUN

6th June: The invasion force includes some 7,000 ships and landing craft manned by over 195,000 naval personnel from eight allied countries. *Notes: The Allies failed to achieve any of their goals on the first day. Carentan, Saint-Lô, and Bayeux remained in German hands, and Caen, a major objective, was not captured until the 21st July. Only two of the beaches (Juno and Gold) were linked on the first day and all five beachheads were not connected until the 12th June, however, the operation gained a foothold that the Allies expanded on over the coming months. German casualties on D-Day have been estimated at 4,000 to 9,000 men. Allied casualties were documented for at least 10,000, with 4,414 confirmed dead. By the 30th June over 850,000 men, 148,000 vehicles and 570,000 tons of supplies had landed on the Normandy shores. Photo: Landing craft disgorge tanks and trucks at Omaha Beach (8th June 1944).*

13th	The first V-1 flying bomb attack on London takes place next to the railway bridge on Grove Road, Mile End. Eight civilians are killed in the blast. *NB: At its peak more than 100 V-1s (also known as buzz bombs or doodlebugs) a day were being fired at southeast England (9,521 in total).*
16th	King George VI visits General Bernard Montgomery's HQ in Normandy.
22nd	The Battle of Kohima in India ends with a victory for British and Indian troops over the Japanese.

JUL

The Ministry of Works builds a small estate off Edward Road, Northolt, to demonstrate prefab houses designed for post-war reconstruction. *Fun facts: Between 1945 and 1951 a total of 156,623 prefab houses were built. Although they were envisaged to last just 10 years a number still survive to this day.*

JUL

3rd	The four-month Battle of Imphal ends with a victory for British and Indian troops after Japanese forces are driven back into Burma. Casualties during the battle include 12,603 Allied troops and 54,879 Japanese troops, killed or wounded. *NB: In a contest run by the British National Army Museum in 2013, voters chose the Battle of Imphal as Britain's Greatest Battle.*
11th	Operation Jupiter: The British VIII Corps takes Hill 112 in a strategic victory over the German Panzer Corps during the Battle of Normandy. *NB: The operation reduces the II SS Panzer Corps to a condition from which it never recovers.*
15th	A riot starts in Park Street, Bristol, after a confrontation between 400 African American GIs and 120-armed U.S. Military Police. The MPs restore control by closing off the street with buses and shooting several GIs in the legs; one rioter is shot dead after stabbing a policeman.

21st July: Winston Churchill makes a 3-day visit to northern France where he meets up with General Bernard Montgomery and British troops. *Photo: General G. G. Symonds, Winston Churchill, General Montgomery and Lieutenant General Miles Dempsey at Caen in Normandy, France (22nd July 1944).*

AUG

3rd	The Education Act 1944, promoted by the President of the Board of Education, Rab Butler, receives Royal assent. The act raises the school leaving age from 14 to 15, and also grants the government the power to raise the age to 16 (which they do on the 1st September 1972). The Act also provides for free full-time education for children between 5 and 15 years of age, and abolishes the marriage bar that had permitted a prohibition on the employment of married women teachers.

AUG

12th — Operation Pluto: In support of Operation Overlord, British engineers, oil companies and the British Armed Forces begin construction of the world's first undersea oil pipelines under the English Channel. Two pipeline systems are laid: one, codenamed "Bambi", from Sandown to Cherbourg, and the other "Dumbo", from Dungeness to Boulogne.

20th August: The American Liberty ship SS Richard Montgomery runs aground off the Nore sandbank in the Thames Estuary, near Sheerness, Kent. The following day as the tide goes down the ship breaks her back. Salvage operations begin and continue until the 25th September 1944 when the ship is finally abandoned. *NB: The wreck of the SS Richard Montgomery remains on the sandbank where she sank. There are still approximately 1,400 tons of explosives on board but the likelihood of explosion is claimed to be remote. Photo: The masts of the sunken SS Richard Montgomery (May 2022).*

21st — The Dumbarton Oaks Conference opens in Washington, D.C. where American, British, Chinese, French and Soviet representatives meet to plan the foundation of what will become the United Nations.

23rd — An American Army Air Force Consolidated B-24 Liberator crashes during a test flight into the centre of the village of Freckleton, Lancashire, killing all three crewmen aboard the aircraft and 58 individuals on the ground, including 38 children aged four to six.

25th — General Dietrich von Choltitz, the military governor of Paris and commander of the German garrison located there, surrenders Paris to the Allies in defiance of Hitler's orders to destroy it.

SEP

1st — General Bernard Montgomery is promoted to field marshal, the highest rank in the British Army.

SEP

3rd	The British Second Army liberates Brussels from German occupation and is welcomed by jubilant crowds of Belgians celebrating in the capital city. Prime Minister Hubert Pierlot's government in exile leaves London five days later and returns to Belgium.

8th September: The first V-2 rocket attack on London takes place striking Staveley Road in the Chiswick district of the city; three people are killed. *Notes: The V-2 rocket was the world's first long-range guided ballistic missile. It travelled at supersonic speed, impacted without audible warning and proved unstoppable as no effective defence existed. Photo: A V-2 rocket ready for launching at Cuxhaven in Lower Saxony (c. 1945).*

11th	Operation Heckle: The Laksevåg floating U-boat dock, at the German-occupied heavily defended Norwegian port of Bergen, is sunk by the British midget submarine X-24.
12th	The Second Quebec Conference (codenamed "OCTAGON") is held Quebec City in Canada. A high-level military conference, the chief representatives are Winston Churchill, Franklin D. Roosevelt and the Combined Chiefs of Staff. Agreements are reached on Allied occupation zones in a defeated Germany, the Morgenthau Plan to demilitarise Germany, continued U.S. Lend-Lease aid to Britain, and the role of the Royal Navy in the war against Japan.
17th	Operation Market Garden: In the largest airborne operation of WWII, Allied paratroopers land in the Netherlands in a failed attempt to capture the Arnhem bridge over the river Rhine.
20th	After three days of fighting British and Empire forces take the occupied neutral microstate of San Marino from the German Army in the Battle of San Marino.
17th	Blackout restrictions, introduced on the 1st September 1939, are relaxed. Lighting can now be used at night as long as it is no brighter than the equivalent of moonlight - full blackout measures are still imposed if an air raid alert is sounded.

SEP

18th	The British submarine HMS Tradewind torpedoes and sinks the Japanese "hell ship" Jun'yō Maru which is carrying approximately 4,200 Javanese slave labourers and 1,450 Allied POWs; over 5,620 are killed, 723 are rescued. *NB: This is one of the highest death tolls of any maritime disaster in World War II, and one of the highest death tolls of any ship sunk by submarine.*
21st	Operation Market Garden: The last British paratroopers at Arnhem Bridge surrender after several days of fighting.

OCT

9th	Prime Minister Winston Churchill and Soviet Premier Joseph Stalin begin a nine-day conference in Moscow to discuss the future of Europe.
10th	The Housing (Temporary Accommodation) Act 1944 receives Royal Assent. *Notes: The Act makes arrangements for post-war provision of adequate housing for all who need it.*
14th	Operation Manna: Following the gradual withdrawal of German occupying forces from Athens, the British 4th and 6th Parachute Battalions march in to the Greek capital.
23rd	The Allies formally recognise the French Committee of National Liberation as the official government of France, with Charles de Gaulle as its leader.

NOV

12th	Operation Catechism: The German battleship Tirpitz is attacked and sunk by RAF Lancaster bombers near Tromsø, Norway. Estimated casualties range from 940 to 1,204.
22nd	The British Technicolor epic film Henry V, produced, directed and starring Laurence Olivier, opens in London. Based on Shakespeare's play, the film achieves both critical and popular acclaim.
25th	A V-2 rocket destroys a Woolworths store on New Cross Road in south east London killing 168 (the highest recorded death toll in Britain from a V-2). *NB: In total there were 1,358 V-2 attacks on London during 1944 and 1945, killing an estimated 2,754 civilians and injuring 6,523 others.*
27th	An accident at the RAF Fauld underground munitions storage depot near Burton upon Trent in Staffordshire causes one of the largest non-nuclear explosions in history, and the largest ever on U.K. soil. Between 3,500 and 4,000 tons of high explosives blow up causing a crater some 30 metres deep and 300 metres in diameter. A nearby reservoir containing 450,000 cubic metres of water is obliterated in the incident, along with several buildings including a complete farm. A total of 70 people are believed to have lost their lives in the explosion and resulting flood, as well as some 200 cattle.
27th	Operation Tigerfish: Freiburg in south west Germany is bombed by 292 RAF Lancaster bombers. A total of 14,525 bombs are dropped on the city killing 2,797 people and injuring approximately 9,600 others.
30th	The Royal Navy battleship HMS Vanguard is launched in a ceremony presided over by Princess Elizabeth. It is the first ship the Princess has ever launched and she is presented with a diamond rose brooch to commemorate the event. *NB: HMS Vanguard was the largest and fastest of the Royal Navy's battleships, and the last to be built.*

DEC

3rd December: The Home Guard is officially stood down following the successful D-Day landings in France and the drive towards Germany by the Allies. A national stand down parade involving 7,000 Home Guard members, representing forces throughout the country, takes place in Central London before His Majesty King George VI. *Fun facts: When Anthony Eden made his broadcast on 14th May 1940 calling for all men between the ages of 17 and 65 to enrol in the Local Defence Volunteers (LDV), within 24 hours 250,000 men had put down their names to join. At its peak in March 1943 the Home Guard numbered over 1,700,000 men - this never dropped below 1 million until the day it disbanded on the 31st December 1945. Extra: The Home Guard earned the nickname "Dad's Army" due to the average age of the volunteers who signed up, many of whom were ineligible for regular military service due to their advancing years. Photo: Chancellor of the Exchequer Sir John Anderson addresses the Civil Service Home Guard on their last parade (3rd December 1944).*

14th	The film National Velvet starring Mickey Rooney and Donald Crisp alongside a young Elizabeth Taylor (in her breakout role as Velvet Brown) is released in the United States.
17th	The city of Ulm in the German state of Baden-Württemberg is heavily bombed by the RAF; 707 people are killed, 613 injured, and 25,000 are left homeless.
19th	The Council of Industrial Design (now the Design Council) is founded by Hugh Dalton, President of the Board of Trade. Its objective is "to promote by all practicable means the improvement of design in the products of British industry".
24th	Heinkel He 111 bombers flying over the Yorkshire coast launch 45 V-1 flying bombs at Manchester. No V-1s actually land in Manchester itself, but 27 people in neighbouring Oldham are killed by a stray bomb. Another 17 people are killed elsewhere and 109 are wounded overall.

Worldwide News & Events

1. 15th January: An earthquake hits San Juan, Argentina, destroying a large part of the provincial capital and killing an estimated 10,000 people. *NB: The earthquake is the worst natural disaster in Argentina's history.*
2. 18th January The Metropolitan Opera House in New York City hosts its first jazz concert. Performers include Louis Armstrong, Billie Holiday and Benny Goodman (via remote hook-up). Attendees of the concert buy war bonds to get a seat and raise $650,000 for the American war effort.
3. 22nd January The Battle of Anzio begins with an Allied amphibious landing (Operation Shingle) in the Lazio region of Italy. Fighting continues until the 5th June when Rome is captured by the Allies. Casualties during the battle include 43,000 Allied troops (7,000 killed, 36,000 wounded or missing), and 35,500 Germans (5,000 killed, 30,500 wounded or missing).
4. 25th January: A total solar eclipse occurs across Peru, Brazil, British Sierra Leon and French West Africa.
5. 27th January: The siege of Leningrad, a military blockade undertaken by the Axis powers on the Eastern Front against the Soviet city of Leningrad (present-day Saint Petersburg), is lifted by the Soviets. *NB: The 872-day blockade was one of the longest and most destructive sieges in history and claimed the lives of 800,000 of the city's inhabitants, mainly through cold and hunger.*
6. 5th February: The black-and-white 15-chapter serial film "Captain America" is released. Starring Dick Purcell, it is the first appearance of a Marvel superhero outside a comic.
7. 7th February Bing Crosby records "Swinging on a Star" with John Scott Trotter and His Orchestra in Los Angeles, California. Introduced in the film Going My Way (1944), it wins an Oscar for Best Original Song at the 17th Academy Awards.
8. 22nd February: The U.S. Army Air Force carry out an opportunistic aerial bombing raid over the Nazi occupied Dutch town of Nijmegen; around 800 civilians are killed.
9. 23rd February: The Soviet authorities begin the forced transfer of the whole of the Vainakh (Chechen and Ingush) populations of the North Caucasus to Kazakhstan and Kyrgyzstan in Central Asia. *NB: Of the 496,000 Chechens and Ingush who were deported (according to Soviet archives) at least a quarter died; Chechen sources put the number of deportees at 650,000.*
10. 24th February: The U.S. Navy fleet submarine USS Rasher torpedoes the Japanese cargo ships Ryusei Maru and Tango Maru, killing 3,000 Javanese labourers and Allied POWs, and 5,000 Imperial Japanese Army soldiers.
11. 29th February: Karol Wojtyla, the future Pope John Paul II, is run down and injured by a Nazi truck in Krakow while walking home from work at a quarry. Wojtyla suffers a severe concussion, numerous cuts and a shoulder injury, and has to spend two weeks in hospital.
12. 2nd March: The 16th Academy Awards ceremony, honouring the best in film for 1943, is held at Grauman's Chinese Theatre in Hollywood. Hosted by Jack Benny, it is the first Oscar ceremony to be held at a large public venue. The winners include director Michael Curtiz and his film Casablanca, Paul Lukas (Best Actor), Jennifer Jones (Best Actress), Charles Coburn (Best Supporting Actor) and Katina Paxinou (Best Supporting Actress). Henry King's The Song of Bernadette receives the most Oscar nominations with 12, and wins the most awards with four.

(2nd March) - Photo: 16th Academy Awards Oscar winners (from left): Paul Lukas, Jennifer Jones, Katina Paxinou and Charles Coburn.

13.	4th March: Louis Buchalter, the mobster and leader of 1930s Mafia hit squad Murder, Inc., is executed at Sing Sing Correctional Facility in the village of Ossining, New York. A few minutes before Buchalter's execution his lieutenants Emanuel "Mendy" Weiss and Louis Capone are also executed.
14.	9th - 10th March: Due to the increase of German activity in Tallinn, Estonia, the Soviet air force begins targeting the city in an effort to debilitate Germany; 757 people are killed and over 20,000 are left homeless.
15.	10th March: Dutch Resistance leader Joop Westerweel is arrested while returning to the Netherlands having escorted a group of Jewish children to safety in Spain. *NB: Westerweel was executed at Herzogenbusch concentration camp on the 11th August 1944.*
16.	15th March: The Soviet Union introduces a new national anthem, the "State Anthem of the USSR", replacing The Internationale.
17.	17th March: Mount Vesuvius in Italy erupts. Over the space of a week and a half, slow-moving lava, rock and ash hail down on the city of San Sebastiano al Vesuvio, destroying it and killing 26 people. *Notes: As the Italian government was in shambles at the time, it was American Allied forces that dealt with the management of evacuating the 7,000 townspeople out of harm's way. NB: The 1944 eruption was the most recent eruption of Mount Vesuvius.*
18.	24th March: Ardeatine massacre: Nazis led by SS officers Herbert Kappler, Erich Priebke and Karl Hass, execute 335 civilians and political prisoners in occupied Rome in retaliation for the previous day's Via Rassela bombing that killed 33 Germans.
19.	27th March: In Sweden, Ruben Rausing files a patent for Erik Wallenberg's tetrahedron-shaped plastic-coated paper carton (used for packaging liquid foods). *NB: This leads to the formation of the Swedish-Swiss company Tetra Pak in 1951.*

| 20. | 1st April: Ascq massacre: Members of the 12th SS Panzer Division Hitlerjugend shoot 86 civilians suspected of blowing up their train on its approach to the Gare d'Ascq in France. |

21. 4th April: The U.S. 15th Air Force sends 215 B-17 and B-24 bombers to begin the Allied bombardment of Bucharest, Romania. *NB: The bombings over Bucharest are carried out over a period of 4 months by the U.S. Air Force and the British Royal Air Force, with approximately 3,640 bombers of different types accompanied by about 1,830 fighters. As collateral damage, 5,524 inhabitants are killed, 3,373 are injured, and 47,974 are left homeless. Photo: 15th Air Force B-24s leave Ploesti (just north of Bucharest) after dropping their bomb loads on the Concordia Vega Oil refinery, the leading oil refinery target in continental Europe, 31st May 1944.*

22.	5th April: Under German guidance, Hungarian authorities require all Jews in Hungary to wear the yellow star. *NB: This order is one of the first of hundreds passed after the Nazi occupation of Hungary to gradually deprive Hungarian Jewish citizens of their civil and human rights.*
23.	10th April: Slovakian Jews Rudolf Vrba and Alfréd Wetzler escape from Auschwitz concentration camp. *Follow up: Between the 25th and 27th April they prepare the Vrba-Wetzler report, one of the earliest and most detailed descriptions of the extermination of Jews at the camp.*
24.	15th April: The self-proclaimed "Philosopher of Fascism" and key figure of Benito Mussolini's Fascist government, Giovanni Gentile, is assassinated in Florence by Bruno Fanciullacci and an associate, both of whom are members of the partisan Gruppi di Azione Patriottica.
25.	19th April: The Japanese launch Operation Ichi-Go, an offensive in central and south China against the National Revolutionary Army of the Republic of China.
26.	22nd April: The German Chancellor Adolf Hitler and the Head of State of the Italian Social Republic Benito Mussolini attend a two-day meeting at Schloss Klessheim near Salzburg in Austria.

(22nd April) - Photo: Hitler and Mussolini greet each other at Salzburg train station ahead of their two-day meeting.

27.	May: Jean-Paul Sartre's existentialist drama No Exit (Huis Clos) premieres in Paris.
28.	1st May: Two hundred Communist prisoners are shot by the Germans at Kaisariani in Athens, Greece, in reprisal for the killing of General Franz Krech by a platoon of the Greek People's Liberation Army.
29.	1st May: American playwright Martin Flavin is awarded the Pulitzer Prize for the Novel for "Journey in the Dark".
30.	3rd May: The film "Going My Way" premieres in New York City. Directed by Leo McCarey and starring Bing Crosby, the musical comedy drama goes on to win seven Oscars (including Best Picture) at the 17th Academy Awards.
31.	6th May: Mohandas Gandhi is released unconditionally from jail in India on health grounds. *NB: Gandhi was arrested by the British under the Defence of India Act on the 9th August 1942 after delivering speech calling for the British to "Quit India".*
32.	12th May: Soviet troops finalise the liberation of the Crimea, forcing German and Romanian forces to evacuate the peninsula.
33.	15th May - 9th July: Under the guidance of the German SS, Hungarian gendarmerie officials deport around 440,000 Jews from Hungary, mostly to Auschwitz-Birkenau where the majority are killed in gas chambers on arrival. *NB: By the end of July 1944 the only Jewish community left in Hungary was that of its capital Budapest.*
34.	30th May: Princess Charlotte Louise Juliette Grimaldi of Monaco renounces and cedes her rights to the throne to her son Prince Rainier Louis Henri Maxence Bertrand Grimaldi (who later reigns as Prince Rainier III of Monaco).
35.	3rd June: The Provisional Government of the French Republic is established, succeeding the French Committee of National Liberation.
36.	4th June: Hunter-Killer Task Group 22.3 captures the German submarine U-505 south of the Cape Verde Islands. *NB: It is the first time since 1815 that an American warship has captured an enemy vessel at sea.*

37. 5th June: Following the German evacuation of Rome a day earlier, Allied troops, under the command of American General Mark Clark, enter the city. *NB: Rome is the first capital of the Axis Powers to fall. Photo: American troops in front of the Vittoria Emmanuel memorial and the Piazza Venezia in Rome, June 1944.*

38.	9th June: The cargo ship SS Tanais (requisitioned by German occupation forces in Greece) is sunk by the Royal Navy submarine HMS Vivid off Heraklion, Crete. Estimates of the number of people killed vary between 425 and 1,000, and include deported Cretan Jews, Cretan Christian civilians and Italian POWs.
39.	10th June: The Soviet leader Joseph Stalin launches the Vyborg-Petrozavodsk Offensive in order to destroy the Finnish Army and to push Finland out of the war.
40.	10th June: The village of Oradour-sur-Glane in Haute-Vienne, France, is destroyed and 643 civilians, including non-combatant men, women, and children, are massacred by a German Waffen-SS company as collective punishment for resistance activity in the area. *Notes: A new village was built after the war on a nearby site but, on the orders of President Charles de Gaulle, the original has been maintained as a permanent memorial.*
41.	17th June: Iceland declares full independence from Denmark.
42.	20th June: MW 18014, a V-2 rocket launched at the Peenemünde Army Research Center in Peenemünde, Germany, becomes the first man-made object to cross the Kármán line into outer space. *Notes: The Kármán line is set by the international record-keeping body FAI (Fédération Aéronautique Internationale) at an altitude of 100 kilometres above mean sea level.*
43.	22nd June: In the U.S. the G.I. Bill, formally known as the Servicemen's Readjustment Act of 1944, is signed into law by President Roosevelt to provide a range of benefits for returning World War II veterans.
44.	22nd June - 19th August: Operation Bagration: A strategic offensive operation by Soviet forces destroys 28 of 34 divisions of the German Army Group Centre and completely shatters the German front line on the Eastern Front.

45.	1st July: The United Nations Monetary and Financial Conference begins at Bretton Woods in the U.S. state of New Hampshire. The conference is attended by 730 delegates from all 44 allied nations to regulate the international monetary and financial order after the conclusion of World War II. The conference ends on the 22nd July and agreements are signed that, after legislative ratification by member governments, lead to the establishment of the International Bank for Reconstruction and Development (IBRD, later part of the World Bank group) and the International Monetary Fund (IMF).
46.	16th July: The first contingent of the Brazilian Expeditionary Force arrives in Naples, Italy, aboard the American Navy transport ship USS General Mann. *NB: The Brazilian troops fought with Allied forces under U.S. command, primarily in the liberation of Italy.*
47.	17th July: The largest convoy of World War II leaves Halifax Harbour, Nova Scotia, under Royal Canadian Navy protection. *Follow up: Convoy HX 300, which includes a total of 159 merchant ships and 32 escorts, arrives safely at British ports on the 3rd August.*
48.	18th July: Hideki Tojo resigns as Prime Minister of Japan due to numerous setbacks in the war effort. He is succeeded by Kuniaki Koiso on the 22nd July.
49.	18th July: Swedish middle distance runner Arne Andersson runs world record 1 mile (4m:1.6s) at Malmo, Sweden, in front of a capacity crowd of 14,000.
50.	20th July: Adolf Hitler survives a plot to assassinate him led by German resistance leader colonel Claus von Stauffenberg at the Wolf's Lair near Rastenburg, East Prussia (now Kętrzyn in present-day Poland). Von Stauffenberg and his fellow conspirators (in this and Operation Valkyrie) are executed the following day.
51.	20th July: American President Franklin D. Roosevelt is renominated for a fourth term at the 1944 Democratic National Convention held at Chicago Stadium in Chicago, Illinois. Missouri Senator Harry S. Truman is selected to be the vice-presidential nominee.
52.	22nd July: The Lublin-Majdanek concentration and extermination camp in Eastern Poland is liberated by the Soviet Red Army. *NB: Captured virtually intact, Majdanek was the first major concentration camp to be liberated. Soviet officials invited journalists to inspect the camp and evidence of the horrors that had occurred there.*
53.	1st August - 2nd October: The Warsaw Uprising, a major operation by the Polish underground resistance to liberate Warsaw from German occupation, begins. Timed to coincide with the retreat of German forces from Poland ahead of the Soviet advance, the Red Army temporarily halted combat operations which enabled the Germans to regroup, defeat the Polish resistance, and to destroy the city in retaliation. Estimations put the number of Polish resistance members killed at around 16,000, and the number of Polish civilians killed at between 150,000 and 200,000, mostly from mass executions. German casualties range between 2,000 and 17,000 soldiers killed and missing. *NB: The Uprising was fought for 63 days with little outside support. It was the single largest military effort undertaken by any European resistance movement during World War II.*
54.	1st August: Anne Frank, a young Jewish girl hiding out in Nazi-occupied Holland, writes her last diary entry. Three days later she and her family are arrested by the Gestapo and placed in concentration camps after a tip-off from a Dutch informer. *Follow up: Anne Frank died in early 1945 from typhus at Germany's Bergen-Belsen concentration camp. Her diary was published by her father in 1947 and has since become a worldwide bestseller.*
55.	2nd August: At the request of Britain, Turkey breaks diplomatic and economic relations with Germany. *NB: On the 23rd February 1945, Turkey declares war on Germany.*

56.	3rd August: At Auschwitz-Birkenau concentration camp 2,897 Gipsies, including men, women and children, are loaded on trucks, taken to gas chamber V and exterminated on the orders of SS Reichsfuehrer Heinrich Himmler. Their bodies are burned in pits next to the crematorium.
57.	4th August: The Finnish Parliament, by derogation, elects Marshal C. G. E. Mannerheim as President of Finland to replace Risto Ryti who has resigned.
58.	5th August: Nearly 400 Japanese internees escape during a mass breakout attempt from a prisoner of war camp near Cowra in New South Wales, Australia. During the escape and ensuing manhunt, 231 Japanese POWs are either killed or commit suicide; four Australian soldiers are also killed during the incident. All the remaining survivors are recaptured within 10 days.
59.	18th August: The French city of Chartres is liberated by the U.S. 5th Infantry and 7th Armored Divisions belonging to the XX Corps commanded by General George S. Patton.
60.	22nd August: Holocaust of Kedros: German Wehrmacht infantry begin an intimidatory razing operation against the civilian residents of nine villages in the Amari Valley on the occupied Greek island of Crete; 164 civilians are massacred.
61.	22nd August: The American submarine USS Bowfin torpedoes and sinks the Japanese passenger ship Tsushima Maru on route to Nagasaki; 1,534 civilians, including 780 schoolchildren, are killed.
62.	23rd August: At Padule di Fucecchio in Tuscany, Italy, members of the German 26th Panzer Division round up 94 men, 63 women and 27 children, and murder them with machine gun fire. The massacre is carried out as a reprisal for the wounding of two soldiers by Italian partisans.
63.	24th August: The American submarine USS Harder is sunk off Luzon in the Philippines by the Japanese minesweeper Kaibokan CD-22; all hands onboard are lost. *Notes: The commanding officer of USS Harder, Samuel D. Dealey, was one of the most decorated American servicemen for valour during World War II. He sunk 16 enemy ships and was awarded the Medal of Honor and four Navy Crosses.*
64.	25th August: The Red Ball Express convoy system begins operation supplying tons of materiel to Allied forces in France. Staffed primarily by African-American soldiers, it runs for 83 days until the 16th November. *NB: At its peak the Express operated 5,958 vehicles that carried around 12,500 tons of supplies a day.*
65.	25th August: Following an ambush a few days earlier, and in reprisals against the activities of the French Resistance, a group of German Waffen SS soldiers enter the village of Maillé in Indre-et-Loire, France, and move from house to house killing men, women and children, and setting everything on fire; 124 of the 500 residents of the commune are killed, including 48 children.
66.	26th August: The leader of the Free French Forces, General Charles de Gaulle, marches at the head of a victory parade down the Champs Élysées in Paris, France, one day after the city's liberation from Nazi occupation.
67.	September: The Dutch famine, also known as the Hunger Winter (from the Dutch Hongerwinter), begins in the German-occupied northern part of the Netherlands. *Notes: Caused by a German blockade that cut off food and fuel shipments, some 4.5 million people were affected; an estimated 18,000 deaths occurred due to the famine.*
68.	1st September: Allied troops enter Belgium.
69.	2nd September: During a bombing mission on the island of Chi Chi Jima, torpedo bomber pilot (and future American President) George H. W. Bush bails out from a burning plane and parachutes into the Pacific Ocean after his squadron is attacked by Japanese anti-aircraft guns. Bush floats for hours on a life raft before being rescued from the water by the U.S. submarine USS Finback.

(26th August) - Photo: General Charles de Gaulle on the Champs-Elysees following the liberation of Paris.

70.	2nd September: The Spanish magazine ¡Hola! is launched in Barcelona.
71.	2nd September: Olavi Laiho, sentenced to death by military court for desertion, espionage and high treason, becomes the last Finn in Finland to be executed.
72.	5th September: The Soviet Union declares war on Bulgaria.
73.	5th September: The transitional Belgium-Netherlands-Luxembourg (Benelux) Customs Convention is signed by the three governments-in-exile in London.
74.	7th September: The American submarine USS Paddle torpedoes and sinks the Japanese hell ship SS Shinyō Maru carrying Allied POWs in the Sulu Sea; 668 American and Allied prisoners are killed, either by the torpedo explosions or by Japanese guards who machine-gun the POWs as they try to escape.
75.	7th September: Members of Vichy France's collaborationist government (under Philippe Pétain) relocate to Sigmaringen in southern Germany.
76.	8th September: The Belgian government in exile returns to Brussels from London.
77.	9th September: In Bulgaria the pro-communist Fatherland Front carries out a coup d'état and declares war on Germany and the other Axis powers.
78.	11th September: An American Army patrol led by Sgt. Warner W. Holzinger becomes the first to cross enemy lines into Nazi Germany.
79.	19th September: German General Hermann-Bernhard Ramcke surrenders the port city of Brest in Brittany, France, after it is surrounded and stormed by the U.S. VIII Corps; 38,000 prisoners are taken.
80.	19th September: An armistice between Finland and the Soviet Union is signed, ending the Continuation War.

81.	22nd September: The Red Army captures Tallinn, Estonia, after the city is abandoned by retreating German forces.
82.	22nd September: President Jose P. Laurel declares the Philippines under martial law through Proclamation No.29 following the bombing of Davao on the 18th September by returning Allied forces. A day later Proclamation No.30 becomes effective declaring the existence of a state of war between the Philippines and the United States & United Kingdom.
83.	6th October: The Battle of Debrecen starts on the Eastern Front in Hungary.
84.	7th October: Members of the Sonderkommando (Jewish work units) in Auschwitz concentration camp stage a revolt killing 3 SS men before being massacred themselves; 450+ prisoners are killed.
85.	10th October: 800 Romani children are systematically murdered at the Auschwitz concentration camp.

86. 12th October: "Columbus Day Riot": Singer Frank Sinatra opens his third season at New York's Paramount Theater and 30,000, mostly teen girls, descend on Times Square. Hundreds of his fans start lining up at midnight for the show and cause a giant commotion outside the theatre. As the day goes on the long lines outside the theatre only lengthen rather than decrease as many of the 3,500 spectators inside refuse to leave after each show. Some of the youngsters faint with hunger and fatigue after sitting over six hours without food, but still refuse to leave until they are bodily removed by the attendants. *Fun fact: Sinatra's fans were coined bobby-soxers because they wore rolled down socks with their saddle shoes and oxfords. Photo: Fans, some waving pictures of Sinatra, being held back by a barrier rope and an usher outside the Paramount Theater in New York City, 12th October 1944.*

87.	14th October: German Field Marshal Erwin Rommel, nicknamed "the Desert Fox", is given the option of facing a public trial for treason as a co-conspirator in the plot to assassinate Adolf Hitler, or to commit suicide by taking cyanide and be buried a hero with full military honours. He chooses the latter.
88.	16th October: Canadian Arctic explorer Henry Larsen returns to Vancouver in the Royal Canadian Mounted Police schooner St. Roch, and in so doing becomes the first person successfully to navigate the Northwest Passage in both directions.
89.	18th October: The Volkssturm Nazi militia is founded on Adolf Hitler's orders. *Notes: The Volkssturm is staffed by conscripting males between the ages of 16 and 60 years who are not already serving in a military unit.*
90.	19th October: A small group of army officers launch a coup in Guatemala beginning the Guatemalan Revolution. The following day the acting President of Guatemala Ponce Vaides surrenders unconditionally.
91.	23rd October: The Battle of Leyte Gulf begins in the waters near the Philippine islands of Leyte, Samar, and Luzon. Over a period of three days U.S. and Australian naval forces decisively defeat the Imperial Japanese Navy in what is the largest naval battle of World War II, and by some criteria the largest naval battle in history. *NB: On the 25th October during the Battle of Leyte Gulf, the Japanese deployed kamikaze suicide bombers against American warships for the first time. Altogether the Allies lost 12 warships and suffered around 3,000 casualties during the battle; the Japanese lost 28 warships and had approximately 12,500 casualties.*
92.	24th October: Captain David McCampbell shoots down 9 Japanese planes in his F6F Hellcat over the Gulf of Leyte and in so doing sets a United States single mission aerial combat record. *Notes: Medal of Honor recipient McCampbell was the third-highest American scoring ace of World War II with 34 aerial victories, and the highest-scoring American ace to survive the war: Major Richard Bong was the country's top flying ace of the war and was credited with shooting down 40 Japanese aircraft.*
93.	25th October: Tone deaf amateur soprano Florence Foster Jenkins, aged 76, makes her debut at Carnegie Hall in New York. Despite never gaining proficiency as a singer (and that's putting it kindly), the recital is a sell-out. When the concert starts laughter bursts forth from the audience leaving "dignified gentlemen" with "tears of mirth streaming down their cheeks." But then they start cheering and clapping, and egging her on. She thinks she is wonderful but is shocked the following day when she is slammed by the press who declare "she can sing everything except notes". Five days later Jenkins suffers a heart attack and she dies a month later... some suggest that it was the scathing reviews that killed her.
94.	31st October: French serial killer Dr Marcel Petiot is apprehended at a Paris Métro station after 7 months on the run. *Follow up: Although Petiot claimed that he had only killed enemies of France, this was dismissed by the judges and jurors at his trial. Petiot was executed by guillotine on the 25th May 1946.*
95.	6th November: The Hanford Site in Benton County, Washington (established in 1943 as part of the Manhattan Project) produces its first plutonium. *NB: Plutonium manufactured at the site was used in the first atomic bomb.*
96.	7th November: Incumbent Democratic President Franklin D. Roosevelt defeats Republican Thomas E. Dewey to win an unprecedented fourth term as President of the United States.
97.	7th November: A passenger train derails due to excessive speed on a declining hill in Aguadilla, Puerto Rico; 16 people are killed and 50 injured.
98.	10th November: The American ammunition ship USS Mount Hood explodes in Seeadler Harbor, Manus Island, Papua New Guinea; 22 small boats are destroyed, 36 nearby ships damaged, 432 men are killed and 371 more injured.

99.	29th November: At Johns Hopkins hospital in Baltimore in the U.S. state of Maryland, Alfred Blalock and Vivien Thomas perform the first heart surgery to correct blue baby syndrome on eighteen-month-old Eileen Saxon.
100.	7th December: Delegates of 52 nations sign the Convention on International Civil Aviation in Chicago, Illinois, creating the International Civil Aviation Organization.
101.	7th December: The Arab Women's Congress of 1944, hosted by the Egyptian Feminist Union in Cairo, formally establishes the Arab Feminist Union.
102.	7th December: An earthquake along the coast of Wakayama Prefecture in Japan causes a tsunami which kills 1223 people.
103.	15th December: A U.S. Army Air Force utility aircraft carrying bandleader Major Glenn Miller disappears in heavy fog over the English Channel while flying to Paris. He is never seen again.
104.	16th December: Germany begins the Ardennes offensive, later known as the Battle of the Bulge. The battle lasts for five weeks and ends in an Allied victory. *NB: The Battle of the Bulge was last major German offensive campaign on the Western Front during World War II.*
105.	17th December: Malmedy massacre: German SS troops under Joachim Peiper machine gun 84 American prisoners of war captured during the Battle of the Bulge near Malmedy, Belgium.
106.	19th December: The French daily newspaper Le Monde begins publication in Paris.

107. 20th December: In the U.S. the Women Airforce Service Pilots (WASP) organization (whose members tested aircraft, ferried aircraft, and trained other pilots) is disbanded. *Photo: Some of the first Women Airforce Service Pilots to ferry B-17 "Flying Fortress" bombers at Lockbourne Army Airfield in Ohio.*

108.	22nd December: The Vietnam People's Army is formed in French Indochina.
109.	24th December: The Belgian troopship SS Léopoldville is sunk in the English Channel by German submarine U-486; approximately 763 soldiers of the U.S. 66th Infantry Division bound for the Battle of the Bulge, and 56 of the ship's crew, drown.
110.	26th December: After 10 weeks of fighting American forces and Filipino guerrillas bring to a conclusion the Battle of Leyte in the Philippines. During the battle a total 3,504 American and 79,261 Japanese (80% from starvation or disease) soldiers are killed. *NB: The decisive victory over the Imperial Japanese Army effectively ends any hope the Japanese have of retaining the Philippines.*
111.	26th December: Tennessee Williams' play "The Glass Menagerie" premieres at the Civic Theatre in Chicago. Championed by Chicago critics Ashton Stevens and Claudia Cassidy, the play moves to the Playhouse Theatre on Broadway on the 31st March 1945, and catapults Williams from obscurity to fame.

BIRTHS

British Personalities

BORN IN 1944

Jimmy Page, OBE
b. 9th January 1944

Guitarist and founder of the rock band Led Zeppelin.

Bobby Ball
b. 28th January 1944
d. 28th October 2020

Comic, actor, singer and television host born Robert Harper.

Geoffrey Hughes, DL
b. 2nd February 1944
d. 27th July 2012

Actor who rose to fame portraying bin man Eddie Yeats on Coronation Street.

Roger Lloyd-Pack
b. 8th February 1944
d. 16th January 2014

Actor best known for playing Trigger in Only Fools and Horses.

Sir Alan Parker, CBE
b. 14th February 1944
d. 31st July 2020

Filmmaker who received the BAFTA Academy Fellowship Award in 2013.

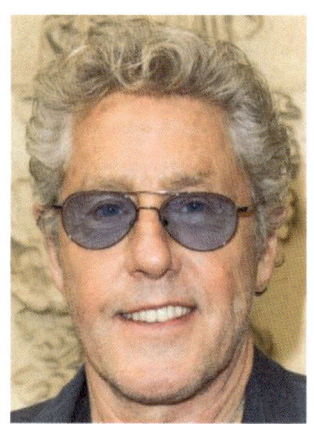

Roger Daltrey, CBE
b. 1st March 1944

Singer, musician, actor and co-founder of the rock band the Who.

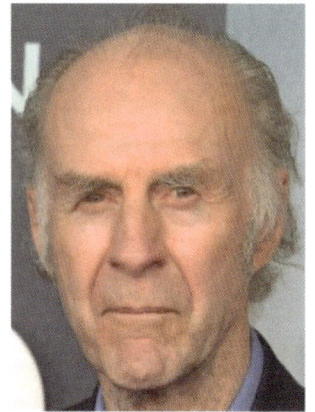

Sir Ranulph Fiennes, OBE
b. 7th March 1944

Explorer, writer and poet, who holds several endurance records.

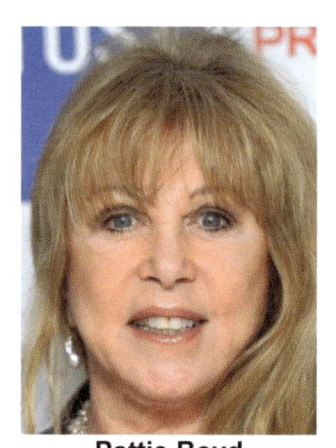

Pattie Boyd
b. 17th March 1944

Model and photographer.

Sir Mike Jackson, GCB, CBE, DSO, DL
b. 21st March 1944

General who served as head of the British Army (2003-2006) during the Iraq War.

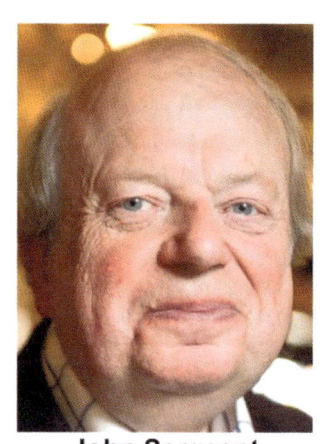

John Sergeant
b. 14th April 1944

Television and radio journalist.

Len Goodman
b. 25th April 1944
d. 22nd April 2023
Ballroom dancer who served as head judge on the BBC's Strictly Come Dancing.

Michael Fish, MBE, FRMetS
b. 27th April 1944

Weather forecaster and presenter for the BBC from 1974 to 2004.

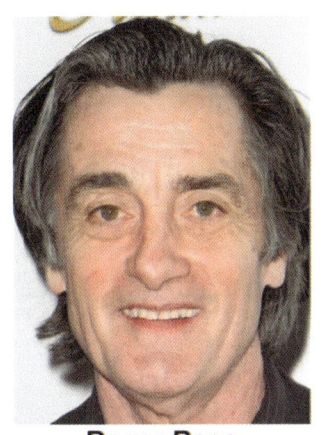

Roger Rees
b. 5th May 1944
d. 10th July 2015
Actor and director who is widely known for his stage work.

John Rhys-Davies
b. 5th May 1944

Actor.

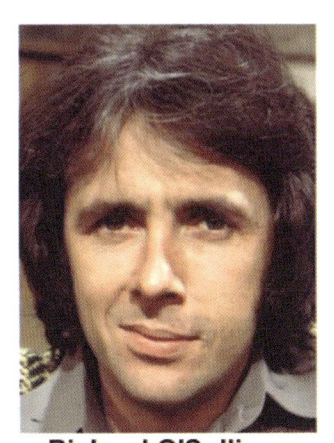

Richard O'Sullivan
b. 7th May 1944

Comedy actor.

Gary Glitter
b. 8th May 1944

Glam rock singer convicted of child sexual abuse in 2006.

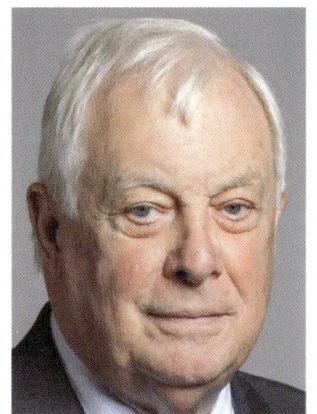

Chris Patten, KG, CH, PC
b. 12th May 1944

Conservative politician who was the 28th and last Governor of Hong Kong.

Joe Cocker, OBE
b. 20th May 1944
d. 22nd December 2014

Singer who released 22 studio albums over a 43-year recording career.

Faith Brown
b. 28th May 1944

Actress, singer, comedian and impressionist.

Robert Powell
b. 1st June 1944

Actor.

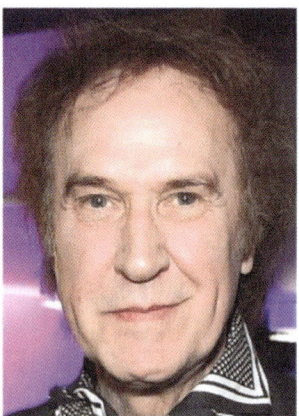

Sir **Ray Davies**, CBE
b. 21st June 1944

Lead vocalist, rhythm guitarist and main songwriter for the rock band the Kinks.

Jeff Beck
b. 24th June 1944

Guitarist who rose to prominence as a member of the rock band the Yardbirds.

Tony Jacklin, CBE
b. 7th July 1944

Golfer who was the most successful British player of his generation.

Rick Davies
b. 22nd July 1944

Musician, singer, songwriter and founder of the rock band Supertramp.

Frances de la Tour
b. 30th July 1944

Actress who has won a Tony Award and three Olivier Awards.

Jonathan Dimbleby
b. 31st July 1944

Television and radio presenter, author and historian.

Ian McDiarmid
b. 11th August 1944

Actor and director of stage and screen.

Jacqueline Bisset
b. 13th September 1944

Actress whose career has spanned over 55 years.

Carol Barnes
b. 13th September 1944
d. 8th March 2008
Television newsreader and broadcaster.

Graham Taylor, OBE
b. 15th September 1944
d. 12th January 2017
Football player, manager, pundit and chairman of Watford Football Club.

Frazer Hines
b. 22nd September 1944

Actor probably best known for his long-running role as Joe Sugden on Emmerdale.

Anne Robinson
b. 26th September 1944

Television presenter and journalist.

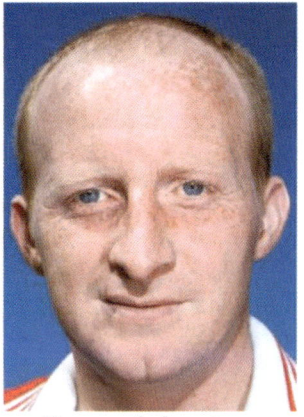

Jimmy Johnstone
b. 30th September 1944
d. 13th March 2006
Footballer who played most of his career for Celtic and won 23 caps for Scotland.

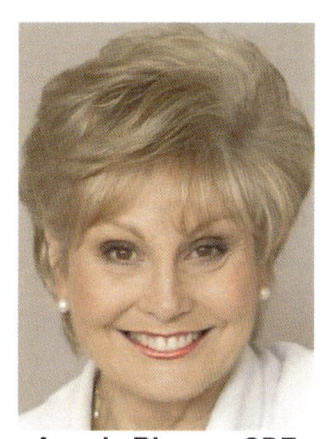

Angela Rippon, CBE
b. 12th October 1944

Television journalist, newsreader, writer and presenter.

Denny Laine
b. 29th October 1944

Musician, singer and songwriter who played with both the Moody Blues and Wings.

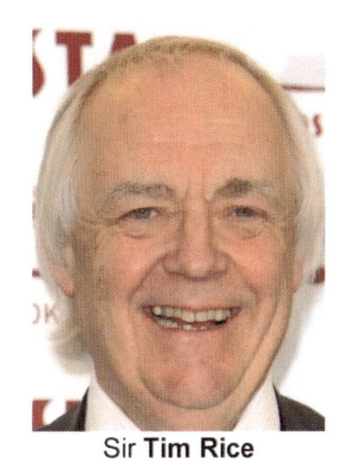

Sir Tim Rice
b. 10th November 1944

Lyricist and author.

Paul Nicholas
b. 3rd December 1944

Actor and singer.

Bernard Hill
b. 17th December 1944

Film and television actor.

Barry Elliott
b. 24th December 1944
d. 5th August 2018
Entertainer who was one half of the comedy duo act the Chuckle Brothers.

Kenny Everett
b. 25th December 1944
d. 4th April 1995
Comedian, radio disc jockey and television presenter.

Notable British Deaths

1st Jan	Sir Edwin Landseer Lutyens, OM, KCIE, PRA, FRIBA (b. 29th March 1869) - Architect who designed many English country houses, war memorials and public buildings.
9th Feb	Agnes Mary Frances Robinson (b. 27th February 1857) - Poet, novelist, essayist, literary critic and translator.
12th Feb	Olive Eleanor Custance (b. 7th February 1874) - Poet who was part of the aesthetic movement of the 1890s and a contributor to The Yellow Book.
12th Feb	Kenneth Cecil Gandar-Dower (b. 31st August 1908) - Sportsman, aviator, explorer and author.
2nd Mar	Ida Smedley Maclean (b. 14th June 1877) - Biochemist who was the first woman admitted to the London Chemical Society.
5th Mar	Alun Lewis (b. 1st July 1915) - One of the best known English language Second World War poets.
19th Mar	Mary Marshall (née Paley; 24th October 1850) - Economist who in 1874 was one of the first women to take the Tripos examination at Cambridge University (although as a woman she was excluded from receiving a degree).
24th Mar	Major General Orde Charles Wingate, DSO & Two Bars (b. 26th February 1903) - Senior Army officer known for his creation of the Chindit deep-penetration missions in Japanese-held territory during the Burma Campaign.
17th Apr	John Thomas Hearne (b. 3rd May 1867) - Middlesex and England medium-fast bowler. His aggregate of 3061 first-class wickets makes him the fourth highest wicket taker in the history of first-class cricket.
8th May	Dame Ethel Mary Smyth, DBE (b. 22nd April 1858) - Composer and a member of the women's suffrage movement. Smyth tended to be marginalised as a 'woman composer', nevertheless she was granted a damehood, the first female composer to be so honoured.
12th May	Commander Harold Godfrey Lowe, RD, RNR (b. 21st November 1882) - The fifth officer on RMS Titanic, the White Star Line passenger liner which sank in 1912. *NB: Lowe was one four officers who survived the disaster.*
12th May	Sir Arthur Thomas Quiller-Couch (b. 21st November 1863) - Writer who published using the pseudonym Q. Although a prolific novelist he is mainly remembered for the monumental publication "The Oxford Book of English Verse 1250-1900" (later extended to 1918) and for his literary criticism.
19th May	Godfrey Wilson (b. 1908) - Anthropologist who studied social change in Africa.
6th Jun	Lieutenant Herbert Denham Brotheridge (b. 8th December 1915) - Army officer who is often considered to be the first Allied soldier to be killed in action on D-Day. He was killed during Operation Tonga: the British airborne landings which secured the left flank of the invasion area before the main assault on the Normandy beaches began.
9th Jun	Keith Castellain Douglas (b. 24th January 1920) - Poet and soldier. Douglas is noted for his war poetry during the Second World War and his memoir of the Western Desert campaign "Alamein to Zem Zem".
24th Jun	Chick Henderson (b. 22nd November 1912) - Singer who achieved popularity and acclaim as a recording artist and performer during the British dance band era.

5th Jul	William Gillies Whittaker (b. 23rd July 1876) - Composer, pedagogue, conductor, musicologist, Bach scholar, publisher and writer.
18th Jul	Thomas Sturge Moore (b. 4th March 1870) - Poet, author and artist.
18th Jul	Reginald John "Rex" Whistler (b. 24th June 1905) - Artist who painted murals and society portraits.
28th Jul	Sir Ralph Howard Fowler, OBE, FRS (b. 17th January 1889) - Physicist and astronomer.
5th Aug	Maurice Joseph Lawson Turnbull (b. 16th March 1906) - Welsh cricketer who played in nine Test matches for the England cricket team between 1930 and 1936. In rugby union he represented Cardiff and London Welsh, and gained two full international caps for Wales in 1933. He also represented Wales at field hockey and was squash champion for South Wales. *Fun fact: Turnbull is the only person to have played cricket for England and rugby for Wales.*
13th Aug	Ethel Lina White (b. 2nd April 1876) - Crime writer best known for her novel The Wheel Spins (1936), on which the Alfred Hitchcock film The Lady Vanishes (1938) is based.
19th Aug	Sir Henry Joseph Wood, CH (b. 3rd March 1869) - Conductor best known for his association with the Proms. He conducted them for nearly half a century introducing hundreds of new works to British audiences.
13th Sep	Noor-un-Nisa Inayat Khan, GC (b. 1st January 1914) - British resistance agent in France during World War II who served in the Special Operations Executive (SOE). As an SOE agent (under the codename Madeleine) she became the first female wireless operator to be sent from the U.K. into occupied France to aid the French Resistance. Inayat Khan was betrayed, captured, and executed at Dachau concentration camp. She was posthumously awarded the George Cross for her service, the highest civilian decoration for gallantry in the United Kingdom.
13th Sep	William Heath Robinson (b. 31st May 1872) - Cartoonist, illustrator and artist best known for drawings of whimsically elaborate machines to achieve simple objectives.

19th September: Wing Commander Guy Penrose Gibson, VC, DSO & Bar, DFC & Bar (b. 12th August 1918) - Distinguished RAF bomber pilot who was the Commanding Officer and leader of 617 Squadron during the "Dambusters Raid" on the Ruhr area of Germany in 1943 (which resulted in the breaching of two large dams). For this he was awarded the Victoria Cross, the highest award for gallantry in the face of the enemy that can be awarded to British and Commonwealth forces. In total Gibson completed over 170 war operations before being killed in action at the age of 26.

20th Sep	Captain John Hollington Grayburn, VC (b. 30th January 1918) - Army officer who was awarded the Victoria Cross for his inspiring leadership and personal bravery in defending the Arnhem road bridge at the Battle of Arnhem.
27th Sep	David Dougall Williams, FRSA (b. June 1888) - Artist and art teacher.
23rd Oct	Charles Glover Barkla, FRS, FRSE (b. 7th June 1877) - Physicist and winner of the Nobel Prize in Physics in 1917 for his work in X-ray spectroscopy and related areas in the study of X-rays.

26th Oct	Princess Beatrice, VA, CI, GCVO, GBE, RRC, GCStJ (b. Beatrice Mary Victoria Feodore; 14th April 1857) - The fifth daughter and youngest child of Queen Victoria and Prince Albert. *NB: Beatrice was the last of Queen Victoria's children to die, nearly 66 years after the first, her elder sister Alice.*
26th Oct	William Temple (b. 15th October 1881) - Anglican priest who served as Bishop of Manchester (1921-1929), Archbishop of York (1929-1942) and Archbishop of Canterbury (1942-1944).
4th Nov	Field Marshal Sir John Greer Dill, GCB, CMG, DSO (b. 25th December 1881) - British Army officer with service in both the First and Second World Wars. From May 1940 to December 1941, he was the Chief of the Imperial General Staff, the professional head of the British Army, and subsequently served in Washington, D.C., as Chief of the British Joint Staff Mission and then Senior British Representative on the Combined Chiefs of Staff.
14th Nov	Air Chief Marshal Sir Trafford Leigh-Mallory, KCB, DSO & Bar (b. 11th July 1892) - Senior commander in the Royal Air Force.
17th Nov	Archibald Campbell MacLaren (b. 1st December 1871) - Cricketer who captained the England cricket team at various times between 1898 and 1909.
22nd Nov	Sir George Clausen, RA, RWS, RI, ROI (b. 18th April 1852) - Artist working in oil and watercolour, etching, mezzotint, drypoint and occasionally lithographs.
22nd Nov	Sir Arthur Stanley Eddington, OM, FRS (b. 28th December 1882) - Astronomer, physicist and mathematician.
30th Nov	Roy Emerton (b. 9th October 1892) - Stage and film actor.
10th Dec	Captain John Henry Cound Brunt, VC, MC (b. 6th December 1922) - Army officer who was awarded the Victoria Cross for his coolness, bravery, devotion to duty and complete disregard of his own personal safety at Faenza during the Italian campaign.
16th Dec	Stuart Paton (b. 23rd July 1883) - Director, screenwriter and actor of the silent era. Paton, who mostly worked with Universal, is accredited with directing 67 films (1915-1938) and writing for 24 films (1914-1927).
16th Dec	Philip Guedalla (b. 12th March 1889) - Barrister, writer and biographer.
26th Dec	George Bellamy (b. 10th July 1866) – Long-time stage actor who went on to appear in 70 films (1911-1933).

POPULAR MUSIC

Bing Crosby	No.1	Swinging On A Star
Bing Crosby & The Andrews Sisters	No.2	Don't Fence Me In
Jimmy Dorsey & His Orchestra	No.3	Besame Mucho
The Mills Brothers	No.4	You Always Hurt The One You Love
The Ink Spots & Ella Fitzgerald	No.5	Into Each Life Some Rain Must Fall
Bing Crosby	No.6	Too-Ra-Loo-Ra-Loo-Ra
Dick Haymes & Helen Forrest	No.7	Together
Frank Sinatra	No.8	A Lovely Way To Spend An Evening
Helen Forrest	No.9	Time Waits For No One
Bert Ambrose & His Orchestra	No.10	I'll Be Seeing You

NB: During this era music was dominated by a number of Big Bands and songs could be attributed to the band leader, the band name, the lead singer, or a combination of these. On top of this the success of a song was tied to the sales of sheet music, so a popular song would often be perfomed by many different combinations of singers and bands and the contemporary charts would list the song without clarifying whose version was the major hit. With this in mind although the above chart has been compiled with best intent it does remain subjective.

Bing Crosby
Swinging On A Star

Label:	Written by:	Length:
Brunswick	Van Heusen / Burke	2 mins 31 secs

Harry Lillis "Bing" Crosby, Jr. (b. 3rd May 1903 - d. 14th October 1977) was a singer and actor who was a leader in record sales, radio ratings and motion picture grosses from 1931 to 1954. Crosby's trademark warm bass-baritone voice made him the best-selling recording artist of the 20th century, selling close to a billion records, tapes, compact discs and digital downloads worldwide. "Swinging on a Star" was introduced by Crosby in the film Going My Way (1944), and won the Oscar for Best Original Song at the 17th Academy Awards.

Bing Crosby & The Andrews Sisters
Don't Fence Me In

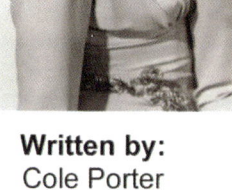

Label:	Written by:	Length:
Decca	Cole Porter	3 mins 7 secs

The Andrews Sisters were a close harmony singing group from the eras of swing and boogie-woogie. The group consisted of three sisters: LaVerne Sophia (b. 6th July 1911 - d. 8th May 1967), Maxene Angelyn (b. 3rd January 1916 - d. 21st October 1995) and Patricia Marie (b. 16th February 1918 - d. 30th January 2013). Throughout their long career the sisters sold well over 75 million records.

Jimmy Dorsey & His Orchestra
Besame Mucho

Label:
Brunswick

Written by:
Consuelo Velazquez

Length:
3 mins 2 secs

James Francis Dorsey (b. 29th February 1904 - d. 12th June 1957) was a jazz clarinettist, saxophonist, composer and big band leader known professionally as Jimmy Dorsey. He was inducted into the Big Band Hall of Fame in 1983 and is considered one of the most important and influential alto saxophone players of the Big Band and Swing era. Dorsey notably played clarinet on the seminal jazz standards Singin' the Blues (1927) and the original recording of Georgia on My Mind (1930), both of which were inducted into the Grammy Hall of Fame.

The Mills Brothers
You Always Hurt The One You Love

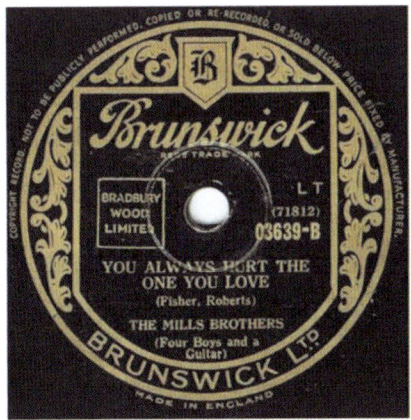

Label:
Brunswick

Written by:
Roberts / Fisher

Length:
3 mins 7 secs

The Mills Brothers, Donald (b. 29th April 1915 - d. 13th November 1999), Harry (b. 9th August 1913 - d. 28th June 1982), Herbert (b. 2nd April 1912 - d. 12th April 1989), and John Jr. (b. 19th October 1910 - d. 23rd January 1936), originally known as the Four Kings of Harmony, were an African-American jazz and pop vocal quartet. They made more than 2,000 recordings and sold more than 50 million records (earning over of three dozen gold records). They were inducted into the Vocal Group Hall of Fame in 1998.

5. The Ink Spots & Ella Fitzgerald
Into Each Life Some Rain Must Fall

Label:	Written by:	Length:
Brunswick	Roberts / Fisher	3 mins 13 secs

The Ink Spots were an African-American Pop vocal group who gained international fame in the 1930s and 1940s. In 1989, the Ink Spots (Bill Kenny, Deek Watson, Charlie Fuqua and Hoppy Jones) were inducted into the Rock and Roll Hall of Fame, and in 1999 they were inducted into the Vocal Group Hall of Fame. "Into Each Life Some Rain Must Fall" featured the Queen of Jazz **Ella Jane Fitzgerald** (b. 25th April 1917 - d. 15th June 1996).

6. Bing Crosby
Too-Ra-Loo-Ra-Loo-Ra

Label:	Written by:	Length:
Decca	James Royce Shannon	3 mins 13 secs

Bing Crosby's intimate singing style influenced many male singers who followed him including Perry Como, Frank Sinatra, Dick Haymes and Dean Martin. For his achievements Crosby has been recognised with three stars on the Hollywood Walk of Fame; for motion pictures, radio, and audio recording.

7. Dick Haymes & Helen Forrest
Together

Label:	Written by:	Length:
Brunswick	Henderson / DeSylva / Brown	3 mins 5 secs

"Together" was included in the film Since You Went Away (1944) and gave rise to this revival of the song with singers **Dick Haymes** (b. 13th September 1918 - d. 28th March 1980) and **Helen Forrest** (b. Helen Fogel; 12th April 1917 - d. 11th July 1999) in a duet. Their recording was paired on a single with "It Had to Be You" which also achieved chart success in 1944.

---

8. Frank Sinatra
A Lovely Way To Spend An Evening

Label:	Written by:	Length:
Columbia	McHugh / Adamson	3 mins 15 secs

Francis Albert "Frank" Sinatra (b. 12th December 1915 - d. 14th May 1998) was a singer, actor, director and producer. During his career he sold more than 150 million records making him one of the best-selling music artists of all time. He also received eleven Grammy Awards including the Trustees, Legend and the Lifetime Achievement Awards.

Helen Forrest
Time Waits For No One

Label:	Written by:	Length:
Decca	Tobias / Friend	3 mins 13 secs

Helen Forrest was an American singer of traditional pop and swing music who, over the course of her career, recorded in excess of 500 songs. During this time Forrest served as the "girl singer" for three of the most popular big bands (Artie Shaw, Benny Goodman, and Harry James) and is regarded by some as the best female vocalist of the Swing Era.

Bert Ambrose & His Orchestra
I'll Be Seeing You

Label:	Written by:	Length:
Decca	Kahal / Fain	2 mins 34 secs

Benjamin Baruch Ambrose (b. 11th September 1896 - d. 11th June 1971), known professionally as Ambrose or Bert Ambrose, was a bandleader and violinist who was the leader of the highly acclaimed British dance band Bert Ambrose & His Orchestra in the 1930s. Although Ambrose retired from performing in 1940, he and his orchestra continued to make records for Decca until 1947.

1944: TOP FILMS

1. **Going My Way** - *Paramount Pictures*
2. **Double Indemnity** - *Paramount Pictures*
3. **Since You Went Away** - *Selznick International Pictures*
4. **Thirty Seconds Over Tokyo** - *Metro-Goldwyn-Mayer*
5. **Meet Me In St. Louis** - *Metro-Goldwyn-Mayer*

OSCARS

Best Picture: Going My Way
Most Nominations: Going My Way / Wilson (10)
Most Wins: Going My Way (7)

Oscar winners (left-right): Barry Fitzgerald, Ingrid Bergman and Bing Crosby.

Best Director: Leo McCarey - *Going My Way*

Best Actor: Bing Crosby - *Going My Way*
Best Actress: Ingrid Bergman - *Gaslight*
Best Supporting Actor: Barry Fitzgerald - *Going My Way*
Best Supporting Actress: Ethel Barrymore - *None But The Lonely*

The 17th Academy Awards, honouring the best in film for 1944, were presented on the 15th March 1945 at Grauman's Chinese Theatre in Hollywood, California.

Directed by: Leo McCarey - Runtime: 2h 6m

When young Father O'Malley arrives at St. Dominic's, old Father Fitzgibbon doesn't think much of the church's newest member.

Starring

Bing Crosby
b. 3rd May 1903
d. 14th October 1977
Character:
Father Chuck O'Malley

Barry Fitzgerald
b. 10th March 1888
d. 4th January 1961
Character:
Father Fitzgibbon

Frank McHugh
b. 23rd May 1898
d. 11th September 1981
Character:
Father Timothy O'Dowd

Trivia

Goofs | In the scene where father O'Malley goes into Carol's apartment you can see a crew member's hand close the door behind him.

Directly after the first rendition of "Going My Way", the shadow of the boom mic can be seen moving on the church wall behind father Fitzgibbon and Miss Linden.

Interesting Facts | Barry Fitzgerald was nominated by the Academy for both the Best Actor and Best Supporting Actor awards for his performance in this film, the only time this has ever happened. Fitzgerald won the Oscar in the supporting category but lost in the lead category to co-star Bing Crosby.

Due to wartime metal shortages Fitzgerald received a plaster Oscar (instead of a gold-plated britannium one) for his performance. A few weeks after he won he broke the head off his plaster Oscar while practicing his golf swing.

The song "Swinging on a Star", sang by Bing Crosby in the film, went on to win the Oscar for Best Song at the 17th Academy Awards. *Fun facts: During his career Crosby sang four different Oscar-winning songs: "Sweet Leilani" (1937), "White Christmas" (1942), "Swinging on a Star" (1944), and "In the Cool, Cool, Cool of the Evening" (1951).*

Quote | *Father Fitzgibbon:* Hope? You know Chuck, when you're young, it's easy to keep the fires of hope burning bright. But at my age, you're lucky if the pilot light doesn't go out.

Double Indemnity

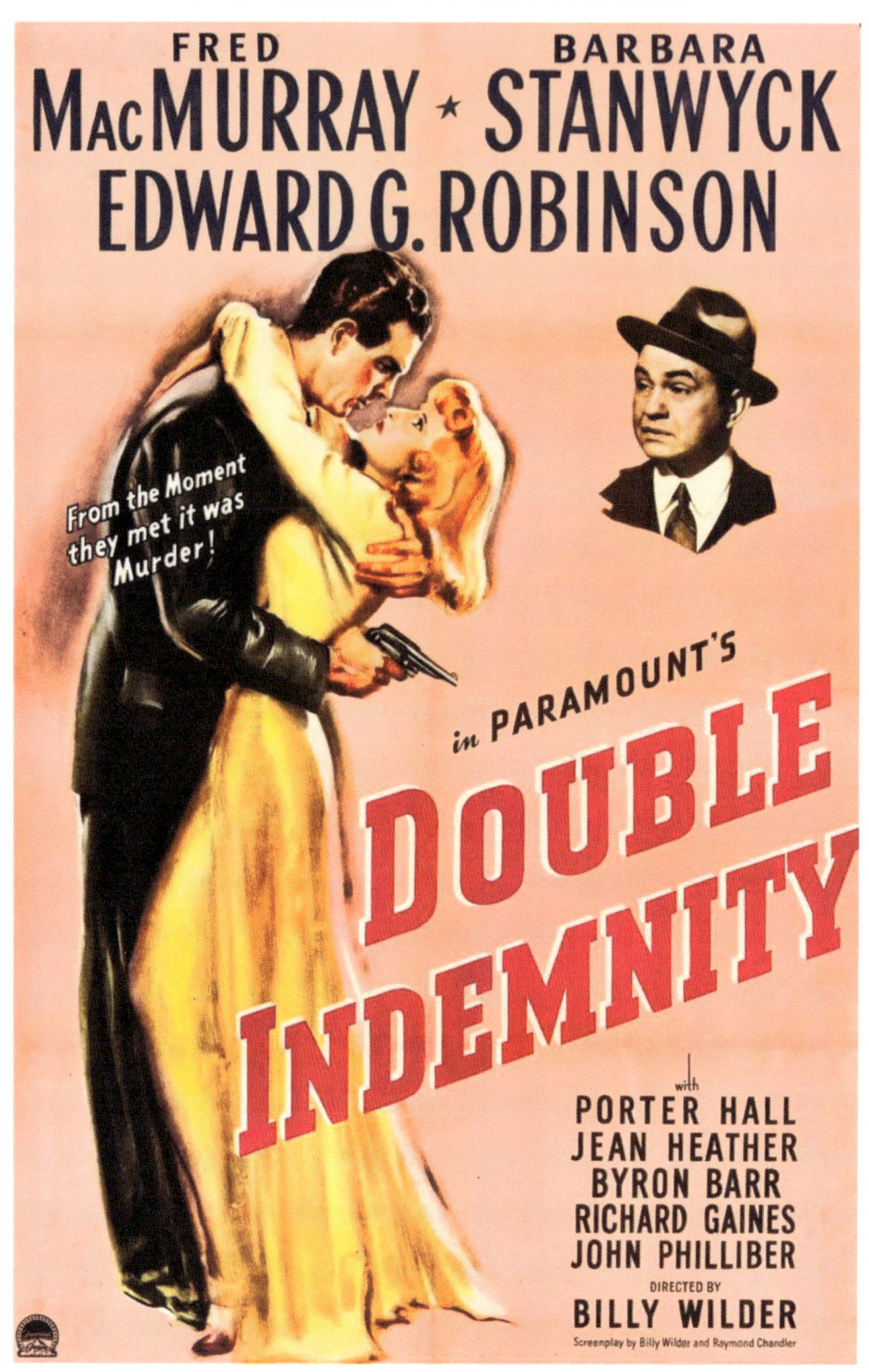

Directed by: Billy Wilder - Runtime: 1h 47m

A Los Angeles insurance representative lets an alluring housewife seduce him into a scheme of insurance fraud and murder that arouses the suspicion of his colleague, an insurance investigator.

Starring

Fred MacMurray
b. 30th August 1908
d. 5th November 1991
Character:
Walter Neff

Barbara Stanwyck
b. 16th July 1907
d. 20th January 1990
Character:
Phyllis Dietrichson

Edward G. Robinson
b. 12th December 1893
d. 26th January 1973
Character:
Barton Keyes

Trivia

Goof | In the first scene in which Walter first kisses Phyllis, we see a wedding ring on Walter's hand. Fred MacMurray was married and the ring was not noticed until post-production.

Interesting Facts | Edward G. Robinson's initial reluctance to sign on for this film was largely because he had been demoted to third lead. Eventually he realised that he was at a transitional phase of his career and that he was getting paid the same as Barbara Stanwyck and Fred MacMurray for doing less work.

When approached about adapting the novel to the screen, Raymond Chandler told director Billy Wilder that he wanted a salary of at least $150 a week and was surprised when producer Joseph Sistrom told the writer that they had planned to give him $750 a week.

The blonde wig that Barbara Stanwyck wears throughout the film was director Billy Wilder's idea. A month into shooting Wilder realised how bad it looked but by then it was too late to re-shoot the earlier scenes. To rationalise this mistake in later interviews Wilder claimed that the bad-looking wig was intentional.

Double Indemnity was selected for preservation into the National Film Registry by the U.S. Library of Congress in 1992 for being "culturally, historically, or aesthetically significant".

Quote | *Phyllis:* I was just fixing some ice tea; would you like a glass?
Walter Neff: Yeah, unless you got a bottle of beer that's not working.

Since You Went Away

DAVID O. SELZNICK Presents the Sensational 8-Star Hit!

CLAUDETTE COLBERT
JENNIFER JONES
JOSEPH COTTEN
SHIRLEY TEMPLE
MONTY WOOLLEY
LIONEL BARRYMORE
ROBERT WALKER
GUY MADISON

Since You Went Away

Directed by: John Cromwell - Runtime: 2h 57m

With her husband away to fight in World War II, a housewife must care for their two daughters alone.

Starring

Claudette Colbert	**Jennifer Jones**	**Joseph Cotten**
b. 13th September 1903	b. 2nd March 1919	b. 15th May 1905
d. 30th July 1996	d. 17th December 2009	d. 6th February 1994
Character:	Character:	Character:
Anne Hilton	Jane Hilton	Lt. Tony Willett

Trivia

Interesting Facts In the film Jennifer Jones and Robert Walker play young lovers. In real life they were at the end of a failed marriage and divorced shortly after. Jones later married David O. Selznick, the producer of this film.

Claudette Colbert originally resisted taking the role of a fortyish mother of a teenager. However, Selznick's insistence that the film would help Wartime morale, and a salary of $150,000, convinced the actress to do it.

At 1 hour, 15 minutes and 38 seconds, Jennifer Jones's performance in this film is the longest ever nominated for an Academy Award for Best Supporting Actress.

Shirley Temple had been in retirement for two years when David O. Selznick persuaded her to join this film. *NB: Since You Went Away was the only Best Picture Oscar nominated film in which Shirley Temple starred.*

At the time, Since You Went Away was the longest and most expensive Hollywood film since David O. Selznick's own Gone with the Wind (1939).

Quote *Jane Hilton:* Mother?
Anne Hilton: Yes, Jane?
Jane Hilton: Mother, do you think I have a nice figure?
Anne Hilton: Yes, darling. You have a beautiful figure.
Jane Hilton: Do you think Tony might paint me someday?
Anne Hilton: Over my dead body.

Thirty Seconds Over Tokyo

M-G-M presents the great motion picture

THIRTY SECONDS OVER TOKYO

A MERVYN LeROY PRODUCTION

with

VAN JOHNSON
ROBERT WALKER
and
SPENCER TRACY

as LIEUTENANT COLONEL JAMES H. DOOLITTLE

Directed by: Mervyn LeRoy - Runtime: 2h 18m

In the wake of Pearl Harbor, a young lieutenant leaves his expectant wife to volunteer for a secret bombing mission which will take the war to the Japanese homeland.

Starring

Spencer Tracy
b. 5th April 1900
d. 10th June 1967
Character:
James H. Doolittle

Van Johnson
b. 25th August 1916
d. 12th December 2008
Character:
Ted Lawson

Robert Walker
b. 13th October 1918
d. 28th August 1951
Character:
David Thatcher

Trivia

Goof | When Ted Lawson's plane lifts off the aircraft carrier deck they immediate raise the landing gear. Several seconds later, when viewed from the side, the landing gear is raised again.

Interesting Facts | When Lawson's plane arrives in Tokyo and sees the fire and smoke from the previous bomber we are not looking at a special effect. During the making of this film there was a fuel-oil fire in Oakland, California, near the filming location. The quick-thinking filmmakers scrambled to fly their camera plane and B-25 through the area, and captured some very real footage in the process.

The weight of one fifty calibre machine gun is roughly equal to that of seven gallons of fuel. In order to reduce weight and increase the B25s range during the real-life Doolittle Raid, the machine guns were removed from the aircraft and replaced with broomsticks that were painted black. The faux guns were intended to discourage enemy fighters from getting too close, which would hopefully reduce the losses of B25s. As this film was released while the war was still on, the broomstick trick was omitted from the film in order to protect the information about the load capacity and range of the B25.

Quote | *Lieutenant Colonel James H. Doolittle:* [on the phone] Hello, hello, York? Dolittle. I want you to get twenty-four B-25's and volunteer crews down to Eglin Field as soon as you can. The job'll take 'em out of the country for about three months. Tell 'em it's a secret mission. They won't know where they're going until they get there. That's right, volunteers. Tell them they're not to talk to anybody. That's an order!

Directed by: Vincente Minnelli - Runtime: 1h 53m

A year in the life of the Smith family leading up to the opening of the in St. Louis World's Fair in the spring of 1904.

Starring

Judy Garland
b. 10th June 1922
d. 22nd June 1969
Character:
Esther Smith

Margaret O'Brien
b. 15th January 1937
Character:
Tootie Smith

Mary Astor
b. 3rd May 1906
d. 25th September 1987
Character:
Mrs. Anna Smith

Trivia

Goofs | When Esther and Tootie perform "Under the Bamboo Tree", Tootie's bedroom slippers are pink at the beginning of the number but change to blue in the "cake walk" finale.

A boom mic shadow is visible on the carriage when the family are leaving to go to the fair.

Interesting Facts | The entire cast and crew were immediately impressed with director Vincente Minnelli's attention to detail in every shot. He had consulted author Sally Benson on how the interiors of the Smith home should look, and she had provided a wealth of first-hand information. As a result, the look of each set was near perfection according to the time period.

Twenty-one-year-old Judy Garland scoffed at the idea of portraying yet another teenager and wanted nothing to do with this film. Her mother even went to MGM chief Louis B. Mayer on her behalf. However, Vincente Minnelli (who she later married) convinced her to play the part of Esther Smith, and Garland later fell in love with the story. In her later years, she considered it one of her favourite roles.

In "Have Yourself a Merry Little Christmas", Judy Garland refused to sing the grim original lyric, "Have yourself a merry little Christmas, it may be your last" to little Margaret O'Brien. The star's creative opposition inspired songwriters Hugh Martin and Ralph Blane to form the more optimistic lyric, "let your heart be light".

Quote | *Tootie Smith*: [after hearing Mr. Smith fall down the stairs] Now I remember where I left my other skate!

Sporting Winners

Football

Between 1939 and 1946 normal competitive football was suspended in England and Scotland as many players had signed up to fight in the war. As a result many teams were depleted and fielded guest players instead.

England: The 1943-1944 season was the fifth season of special wartime football in England. The Football League and FA Cup were suspended and replaced with regional competitions. Appearances in these tournaments did not count in players' official records.

Competition	Winner
League South	Tottenham Hotspur
League West	Lovell's Athletic
League North	Blackpool (1st Championship)
	Bath City (2nd Championship)
League North Cup	Wrexham
Football League War Cup	Aston Villa (Northern Section)
	Charlton Athletic (Southern Section)
	Villa and Charlton drew 1-1 in a playoff

Scotland: The 1943-1944 season was the fifth season of special wartime football in Scotland. The Scottish Football League and Scottish Cup were suspended and replaced with regional competitions. Appearances in these tournaments did not count in players' official records.

Competition	Winner
Southern League	Rangers
North-Eastern League (Autumn)	Raith Rovers
North-Eastern League (Spring)	Aberdeen
Glasgow Cup	Rangers
Renfrewshire Cup	St Mirren
Southern League Cup	Hibernian
Summer Cup	Motherwell
North-Eastern League Cup (Autumn)	Rangers
North-Eastern League Cup (Spring)	Rangers
East of Scotland Shield	Hearts

International Matches

Five unofficial international football matches were played in 1944 between England, Scotland and Wales. During this period no caps were awarded.

Date	Team	Score	Team	Location
19th Feb	England	6-2	Scotland	London
22nd Apr	Scotland	2-3	England	Glasgow
6th May	Wales	0-2	England	Cardiff
16th Sep	England	2-2	Wales	Liverpool
14th Oct	England	6-2	Scotland	London

Rugby - Home Nations

The 1944 Home Nations Championship series was not contested due to the war. International rugby was put on hold and would not resume again until 1947, when the Home Nations would become the Five Nations with the addition of France to the line-up.

Horse Racing

Grand National: Although the Grand National was run as normal in 1940 and most other major horse races around the world were able to be held throughout the war, the commandeering of Aintree for defence use in 1941 meant the Grand National could not be held between 1941 and 1945.

The Derby Stakes is Britain's richest horse race and the most prestigious of the country's five Classics. First run in 1780 this Group 1 flat horse race is open to three year old thoroughbred colts and fillies. Although the race usually takes place at Epsom Downs in Surrey, during both World Wars the venue was changed and the Derby was run at Newmarket - these races are known as the "New Derby". *Note: Epsom Downs racecourse was used for an anti-aircraft battery throughout World War II.*

Ocean Swell Derby 1944
Churchill 'A' Series

Winner	Jockey	Trainer	Owner	Prize Money
Ocean Swell	Billy Nevett	Jack Jarvis	6th Earl of Rosebery	£5,901

Golf - Open Championship

The Open Championship was not held in 1944 due to the war and would not be contested again until 1946.

Tennis - Wimbledon

The 1944 Wimbledon Championships was another sporting event cancelled due to World War II. Hosted since 1877 by the All England Lawn Tennis and Croquet Club in Wimbledon, London, the competition did not resume again until 1946.

County Cricket

All first-class cricket was cancelled during the Second World War. No first-class matches were played in England after Friday, 1st September 1939. Cricket would resume again on Saturday, 19th May 1945.

World Snooker Championship

The World Snooker Championship was cancelled because of the war and would not be held again until 1946.

The Cost Of Living

Comparison Chart

	1944	1944 (+ Inflation)	2023	% Change
3 Bedroom House	£1,500	£81,243	£281,272	+246.2%
Weekly Income	£3.7s.10d	£183.70	£640	+248.4%
Pint Of Beer	9d	£2.03	£4.19	+106.4%
Cheese (lb)	1s.9d	£4.74	£3.23	-31.9%
Bacon (lb)	1s.11d	£5.19	£3.79	-27.0%
The Beano	2d	45p	£2.99	+664.4%

In Peace time it is 'Golden Shred'

Now it's J.R JELLY MARMALADE

Why? Because war conditions restrict supplies of bitter oranges which prevents the manufacture of "GOLDEN SHRED." Fruit is controlled, but *quality* cannot be standardised. Robertson's pre-war reputation and skill, coupled with our 80 years' old tradition, still count for a lot.

It's a Robertson Product —you can depend on it

CREATED BY A MASTER

BATH ESSENCE

PERFUME

LIPSTICK

FACE POWDER

GOYA
LONDON, W.1

Shopping

Weetabix (small size)	7½d
Brooke Bond Dividend Tea (½lb)	1s.7d
Quaker Malted Wheat Flakes (pkt.)	5½d
Bospur Gravy Powder (pkt.)	2d
Brand's Baby Foods (bottle)	7½d
Palmolive Soap (tablet)	4d
Macleans Shaving Cream (jar)	1s.3d
Lever's Easy Shaving Stick	7½d
Goya Lipstick	7s.6d
Tek Toothbrush (nylon)	1s.6d
Pepsodent Toothpaste	1s.3d
Kolynos Denture Fixative	1s.3d
Yeast-Vite (bottle)	1s.4d
Jennings' Ointment (tin)	1s.3d
Fynnon Salt (large tin)	1s.6d
Beecham's Powders (x8)	1s.4d
Pineate Honey Cough Syrup	1s.9d
Aspro (5 tablets)	3½d
Koray Pain Killers (5 tablets)	3½d
Maclean's Stomach Tablets	7d
Potter's Asthma Cure	2s.2d
Crooke's Halibut Oil (100 capsules)	8s.6d
Softex Toilet Roll	1s.3d
Oxydol Granulated Washing Soap	3½d
Sanitas Antiseptic	1s.1½d
Buffle Insect Powder	1s

Gibbs COLD CREAM SOAP soothes Baby's skin

Now baby-creams are scarce, Gibbs Cold Cream Soap is more than ever necessary for Baby. This soap is not only specially mild, but it is so richly creamy that it helps to protect from chafing and soreness. See that your baby has the comfort of Gibbs Cold Cream Soap.

D. & W. GIBBS

COLD CREAM SOAP

D. & W. GIBBS, LTD., LONDON, E.C.4   7½D Including Purchase Tax

LET'S HAVE A GIN AND VOTRIX

VOTRIX VERMOUTH Sweet **7/-** or Dry **7/6**

Vine Products Ltd. cannot supply you direct, so please ask your usual supplier

Mother! Child's Best Laxative is 'California Syrup of Figs'

When your child is constipated, bilious, has colic or diarrhœa, a teaspoonful of 'California Syrup of Figs' brand laxative sweetens the stomach and promptly cleans the bowels of poisons, souring food and waste. Never cramps or over- acts. Children love its delicious taste.

Ask for 'California Syrup of Figs,' which has full directions for infants in arms and for children of all ages. Obtainable everywhere, 1/4 and 2/6. Mother! You must say 'CALIFORNIA.'

Other Items

Sunbeam Bicycle	£9.12s.1d
Rego Tailored-To-Measure Utility Suit	£4.5s
Evans Oxford Street Frock	£3.7s.2d
Three Castles Cigarettes (20)	2s.8d
Richmond Gem Cigarettes (20)	2s.4d
Goya Perfume	£3.10s
Woman's Weekly Magazine	3d
Daily Express Newspaper	1d
Daily Mirror Newspaper	1d

HOUSEWIFE 1944

The Hand that held the Hoover works the Lathe!

With no glamour of uniform, with all the burdens and responsibilities of running a home, thousands of housewives in 1944 are war-workers too. They are doing a double job. They get no medals for it. But if ever women deserved especial honour, these do. So to all war-workers who also tackle shopping queues, cooking, cleaning, mending and the hundred and one other household jobs

Salute! FROM HOOVER

Hoover users know best what improvements they would like in the post-war Hoover. Suggestions are welcome.

BY APPOINTMENT TO H.M. KING GEORGE VI AND H.M. QUEEN MARY
HOOVER LIMITED, PERIVALE, GREENFORD, MIDDLESEX

Money Conversion Table

Pounds / Shillings / Pence 'Old Money'	Decimal Value	Value 2023 (Rounded)
Farthing	¼d	0.1p	6p
Half Penny	½d	0.21p	11p
Penny	1d	0.42p	23p
Threepence	3d	1.25p	68p
Sixpence	6d	2.5p	£1.35
Shilling	1s	5p	£2.71
Florin	2s	10p	£5.42
Half Crown	2s.6d	12.5p	£6.77
Crown	5s	25p	£13.54
Ten Shillings	10s	50p	£27.08
Pound	20s	£1	£54.16
Guinea	21s	£1.05	£56.87
Five Pounds	£5	£5	£270.81
Ten Pounds	£10	£10	£541.62

SITUATIONS VACANT

Minimum Pre-Paid Charge for ALL Small Adverts. 20 words 3/-; 28 words 4/-; 36 words 5/- (Otherwise 1/- Per Line Per Week)

NIGHT WORKERS

Men - - 1/11 per hour
Women 1/6 ,, ,,

Sunday to Friday inclusive, 11p.m. to 8a.m.

Machine cleaning in Food Factory.

*Pleasant surroundings. Good Canteen.
Excellent A.R.P. Shelters.*

This announcement does not apply to a woman between the ages of 18 and 41 unless she has a child of her own under the age of 14 living with her.

Apply: Staff Officer,
HENRY TELFER Ltd.,
82 LILLIE ROAD,
FULHAM, S.W.6.

COW & GATE MILK FOOD
"Babies Love it!"

Printed in Great Britain
by Amazon